Contents

SKELTON N.
SKELTON-ON
RIPON
HG4 5AJ

Name: _____

1) Your handwriting folder

Use your best handwriting to design a cover for your handwriting folder.
Make a Title box and add your name and the date started.
Then you may decorate the borders.

Think about this!

Exercise books and files often look very similar. By covering your books and files and decorating the covers, you can personalise them and make them last longer.

Decorative patterns

Here are some patterns that you might use to decorate your work.
Try these first and then design some patterns of your own.

3 Lost, stolen or strayed?

Some people like to write a label in all their books to make sure that people who borrow them, return them. Your label might include a logo of your intertwined initials.

From the library of

This book belongs to

_____

_____

It was bought on

_____

_____

4 My handwriting:
A checklist

Use this checklist to think about your handwriting.
You may discuss your answers with your partner, if you wish.

Presentation

Can other people read your handwriting?	Yes No
Does your handwriting look neat?	Yes No
Do all your titles and headings stand out clearly?	Yes No
Does your handwriting slope ...	
to the left?	Yes No
to the right?	Yes No
all over the place?	Yes No
Can you judge the space you will need for titles and headings?	Yes No
Do you have a special pen that you prefer to write with?	Yes No
Has your best handwriting improved since last year?	Yes No

Style

Do most of your letters join?	Yes No
If you don't put your name on your page, is your handwriting still recognisable as yours?	Yes No
Do you have a distinctive signature?	Yes No
Does your handwriting flow easily?	Yes No
Do you have one style for notes and another for presentational writing?	Yes No

Sustained work

Can you produce legible handwriting when writing quickly?	Yes No
If you write a long piece of work, does your handwriting get worse towards the end?	Yes No
What action do you think you need to take to improve your handwriting?	

5 All about me!

Use the set of lines below to write as much as you can about yourself. You might use the lines to make a rough draft, which you then copy out neatly and store in your handwriting folder.

_____

_____

_____

_____

_____

_____

_____

_____

_____

_____

_____

_____

_____

_____

_____

_____

_____

_____

_____

_____

Here is the web page for the company that publishes this book.
Web page headings must be clear and catch the eye. Make sure to look at
other web sites to see how printed handwriting is used for effect.

Shop signs use many different letter styles in various shapes and sizes, as the examples below illustrate. Write what you think could be bought in each of these shops. On separate sheets of paper, design and colour three signs for shops. Make sure you use different letter styles and sizes for each sign. You can add decorative borders and motifs, if you wish.

8 Designing labels

People use decorative lettering to label items in their garden.
Design some labels for the vegetables listed below, then decorate
the borders of each label.

Think about this!

Sometimes it is a good idea to first make a pencil draft
to check how long a label should be.

Carrot Parsnip Cauliflower Onion Cabbage Pea
Runner Bean Potato

Decorating letters

Write and decorate the capital letters needed to complete
the days of the week.

onday

uesday

ednesday

hursday

riday

aturday

unday

10 Decorating letters

Write and decorate the capital letters needed to complete the names of the other eight planets in our solar system that orbit the Sun.

enus

upiter

aturn

ercury

ranus

ars

luto

eptune

11 Captions for photographs

Keeping special photographs in an album and labelling them helps you to remember when they were taken. Copy out the photo captions below.

Our kittens Pip, Bubble and Squeak: born 15th April 2000.

_____

_____

_____

A mother bear and her cubs: London Zoo, 20th July 2000.

_____

_____

_____

A very hairy Highland cow: Aviemore, 4th September 1999.

_____

_____

Two swans flying away: Norfolk Broads, 3rd March 2000.

_____

_____

Handwriting check 1:
"Beowulf"

Copy part or all of this extract in your best handwriting.
You might use your Handwriting folder to store extracts from your
favourite stories or information books.

Think about this!

You may wish to **enlarge**, *italicise* or <u>underline</u> words
to enhance their impact.
Look at a range of texts to see how various other authors
use punctuation for effect.

Through the dark night a darker shape slid.
A sinister figure shrithed down from
the moors, over high shoulders, sopping tussocks,
over sheep-runs, over gurgling streams.
It shrithed towards the timbered hall, huge
and hairy slightly stooping. Its long arms
swung loosely ...
Through half-closed eyes Beowulf was
watching, and through barred teeth he
breathed one word. "Grendel." The name of
the monster, the loathsome syllables ...
Grendel saw the knot of sleeping men and
his eyes shone with an unearthly light.
He lurched towards the nearest man, a brave
Geat called Leofric, scooped him up and,
with one ghastly claw, choked the scream in
his throat. Then the monster ripped him
apart, bit into his body, drank the blood
from his veins, devoured huge pieces; within
one minute he had swallowed the whole
man, even his feet and hands.

Handwriting check 2:
"Gruesome"

Write this poem in your best handwriting and store it in your Handwriting folder.
You might like to keep some more poems ready in case you need them.

I was sitting in the sitting room
toying with some toys
when from a door marked: "Gruesome"
There came a GRUESOME noise.

Cautiously I opened it
and there to my surprise
a little GRUE lay sitting
with tears in its eyes.

"Oh little GRUE please tell me
what is it ails you so?"
"Well I'm so small," he sobbed,
"GRUESSES don't want to know."

"Exercises are the answer,
Each morning you must DO SOME."
He thanked me, smiled,
and do you know what?
The very next day he ...

Roger McGough

Designing and labelling illustrations

Design your own fiend as an illustration for a ghost story.
Label the different parts of your fiend to show what makes it really scary!
Remember to include the colours for the illustrator.

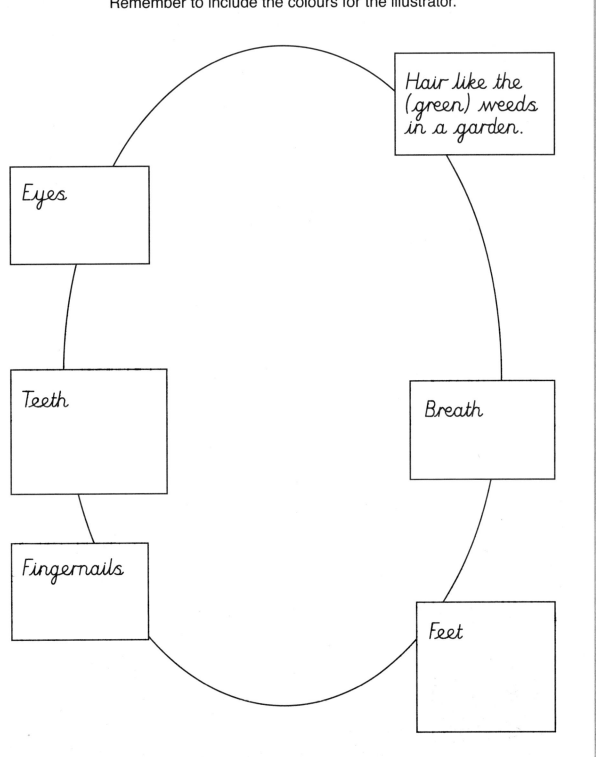

Hair like the (green) weeds in a garden.

Eyes

Teeth

Fingernails

Breath

Feet

Some words you should know

Write the words in the box in alphabetical order. Then practise reading and spelling them with your partner.

Think about this!

Practise writing each word several times.
You may want to write them in different styles to create a dramatic effect.

Frankenstein beast doppelganger vampire creature fiend ghost transmogrifier Dracula ghoul demon werewolf monstrosity

Some words you should know

Write the words in the box in alphabetical order. Then practise reading and spelling them with your partner.

Think about this! Practise writing each word several times.
You may want to write them in different styles to create a dramatic effect.
When you have practised writing each word, try to find an example of it and design a poster to show what the word means.

obituary haiku epitaph rhyme tanka anecdote
kenning saga ballad proverb limerick
metaphor mnemonic

Write this poem in your best handwriting. You might wish
to decorate it with scary images from the poem!

I don't believe in vampires,
I'll say it loud and clear,
I don't believe in werewolves,
When other folk are near.

I certainly don't believe in ghosts,
All those that do are fools,
And I know for an absolute positive fact,
There are no such things as ghouls.

So why, when it is late at night,
After all that I've just said,
Do vampires, werewolves, ghosts and ghouls
All gather underneath my bed?

The truth, of course, is obvious,
And plain for all to see,
For though I don't believe in them,
They all believe in me!

Willis Hall

As well as storing poems in your Handwriting folder, you may wish to compile your own anthology of favourite poems. Collect poems that match the categories below.

Think about this!

When you are compiling your anthology, you will need to use a colon, semi-colons or commas to separate titles.

Rhymes and Jingles

Playground Rhymes

Humorous Verse

Ballads, Sagas and Epic Poems

Sinister and Weird

Shape Poems

Limericks and Poetic Jokes

Beautiful, but Sad

Tanka

Well-known Favourites

Haiku

Romantic Verse

Write this extract, but make sure to insert the correct punctuation.

Think about this! Think carefully about where commas might be placed in the extract. You might also wish to use dashes or brackets to emphasise meaning.

for most of the rest of the morning mr barrack read out loud to the boys pacing up and down as he did so the candle flames fluttered in his wake and his black shadow danced on the walls curled in his hand was the end of a knotted rope which he swung as he walked striking it across a desk from time to time to make the boys jump awake every now and then he stopped and pointed at a boy who had to stand up and recite the sentences hed just heard if he got it wrong mr barrack swung the knotted end of the rope across the boys hand

Berlie Doherty

Read through this letter of complaint and then write your own letter to a newspaper, complaining about something that annoys you.

To: The Editor

Dear Sir/Madam,

I am writing to complain about the behaviour of the young children and teenagers in my area. Yesterday, I went to visit an elderly neighbour who is terrified to go out of her house. She has been plagued by the children on her estate, putting rubbish through her letter box, calling names after her when she goes to the shop and now throwing stones at her windows.

Do the parents of these children know what they are up to? Are all children so rude and ill-mannered? My own children are now grown-up but I don't remember them getting into this sort of trouble! I understand that children want to be with their friends but do they need to hang around on street corners and harass the elderly? In my day, children were taught to be seen and not heard!

I hope that if you would be so kind as to print this letter in your newspaper, the parents concerned might take some action to stop this problem.

Yours faithfully,

Brenda Blenkinsop (Mrs)

The Editor of the newspaper asked his own young son what he thought about the letter on sheet 20. Here are some of the points he made in reply. What points would you make? Set them out as bullet points, making sure to use the correct punctuation.

Dad,

There is no excuse for being rude and unkind to other people, but:

- The young people in this area have nowhere to go in the evenings;
- In summer we can go to the park, but this is no good in winter and our parents like us to stay near to the house;
- You can go to the pub for a drink but we have nowhere to meet;
- We like to talk privately but we can't do that in someone's house. Besides, no one has room for us;
- We do not mean to be threatening, but often when we laugh and joke, people think we are laughing at them;
- Old people can be just as rude as young people;
- Once we have done our homework, we want to do something interesting and have some fun;
- If we use our skates, skateboards or bikes, in the streets we get accused of knocking people down;
- The young children have an adventure playground but we are too old to use it;
- There used to be a Youth Club but it had to close through lack of funding.

I hope some of these points help to answer the lady's complaints. I must rush now because I want to finish my homework and go out with my mates!

Your ever loving son.

22 Designing a play area

The Editor's son made a plan of what he would like to see in a play area for older children. If you could design a play area, what would it contain? Here are some of the things you might want to include.

Think about this!

How might you use arrows, dashes and brackets to make your meaning clear?

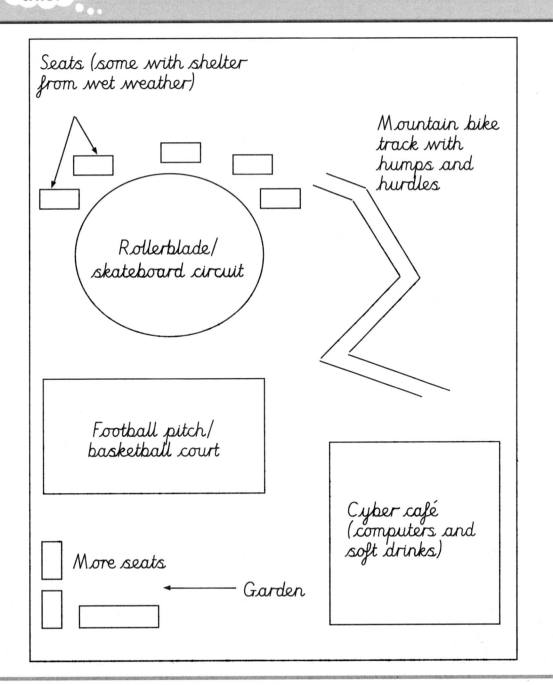

Seats (some with shelter from wet weather)

Mountain bike track with humps and hurdles

Rollerblade/ skateboard circuit

Football pitch/ basketball court

Cyber café (computers and soft drinks)

More seats

Garden

23 Writing a letter to your local council

Compose and write a letter to your local council, asking them to consider providing a play area for older children.

Think about this! You may want to write a first draft and then work as a group to compose a final version.

Here are some points you might like to remember.

1. How should you address a councillor?

2. Remember: a polite request is more likely to be considered than a demand!

3. Is there an area of waste ground that might be suitable for use?

4. Remember to enclose your plans. How will you make sure the councillors don't ignore them?

5. The council may want to help but may not have any money. How might you raise some of the money?

6. Remember to thank the councillors for reading and considering your letter.

Can you think of any other points you should consider when writing a letter to your local council? Write them here.

_____

_____

_____

_____

_____

24 Proverbs and sayings

Write these proverbs and sayings and then practise reading and spelling them with your partner.

Think about this!

A proverb is a witty saying that tells a truth about the way we live.
Find a reference book of proverbs and copy out some of your favourites.

A bad workman always blames his tools.

_____

_____

_____

A drowning man will clutch at a straw.

_____

_____

_____

A friend in need is a friend indeed.

_____

_____

_____

A hungry man is an angry man.

_____

_____

_____

Some words you should know

Write the words in the box in alphabetical order. Then practise reading and spelling them with your partner.

Think about this!

Practise writing each word several times.
You may want to write them in different styles to create dramatic effect.

autobiography glossary commentary hypothesis alliteration synopsis parody assonance narration biography appendix

26 A passage to punctuate:
"The dark is rising"

Write this extract, making sure you insert the correct punctuation.

the old ones stood in the doorway of the church their arms linked together none spoke a word to another wild noise and turbulence rose outside the light darkened the wind howled and whined the snow whirled in and whipped their faces with white chips of ice and suddenly the rooks were in the snow hundreds of them black flurries of malevolence cawing and croaking diving down at the porch in shrieking attack and then swooping up away

Susan Cooper

Captions for cartoons

Draw some cartoons to illustrate these witty sayings.
Then write an informative caption beneath each image.

Don't throw the baby out
with the bathwater.

_____

_____

_____

Take the bull by the horns.

_____

_____

_____

I'll believe that when pigs
fly.

_____

_____

_____

The pen is mightier than
the sword.

_____

_____

_____

People often use decorative lettering to label plants in their garden.
Design some labels for the flowers listed below, then decorate
the borders of each label.

Rose Dahlia Rhododendron Daisy Daffodil Iris
Geranium Tulip Lily Chrysanthemum

Write this poem in your best handwriting.

I wandered lonely as a cloud
That floats on high o'er vales and hills,
When all at once I saw a crowd,
A host of golden daffodils,
Beside the lake, beneath the trees
Fluttering and dancing in the breeze.

Continuous as the stars that shine
And twinkle on the Milky Way,
They stretched in never-ending line
Along the margin of the bay;
Ten thousand saw I at a glance
Tossing their heads in sprightly dance.

The waves beside them danced, but they
Outdid the sparkling waves in glee:
A poet could not but be gay
In such a jocund company!
I gazed – and gazed – but little thought
What wealth the show to me had brought.

For oft, when on my couch I lie
In vacant, or in pensive mood,
They flash upon that inward eye
Which is the bliss of solitude;
And then my heart with pleasure fills,
And dances with the daffodils.

William Wordsworth

Design an illustration for each of the following sayings and write the relevant proverb underneath.

Great minds think alike.

Two wrongs don't make a right.

People in glass houses shouldn't throw stones.

_____

_____

_____

_____

_____

_____

_____

_____

_____

Think about this!

These sayings are not intended to be taken literally. They have a double meaning. We use them to make a point. Think about how you might illustrate "There's many a slip 'twixt cup and lip!"

We all like to receive invitations to parties. If you were having a party, what would you put on the invitations to be sent out? Use the example below to help you design an invitation to your party.

You are invited to:

A Disco and Hot-pot Supper

with music by

The Pickled Onions

on

Tuesday 30th September

at 7:30pm

Please wear your best "bib and tucker".

Write a short description of your favourite party. The questions below might give you some ideas.

Would you have your party at home or somewhere else?

_____

Would you have your party in a different country?

_____

At what time of the year would it be held?

_____

Would you have it during the week or at the weekend?

_____

Would you choose a theme, e.g. fancy dress?

_____

How would you provide the music? Would a famous group play?

_____

_____

What kind of food would you have?

_____

_____

Would you play party games?

_____

Would you invite lots of people or only a special few?

_____

33 Rules of behaviour for pupils

Write the rules listed below as a poster for display in your classroom. Decide whether you think the rules should be written in print or joined writing. You may decorate your poster, if you wish.

Rules of behaviour

1. Do not run in the corridors.
2. Do not talk during Assembly.
3. Do not chew gum in class.
4. Do not leave the classroom without permission from your teacher.
5. Do not drop litter in the playground.

Think about this!

Rules are called imperatives: they must be obeyed. Often they are there to ensure our safety.
Write a list of rules to help a young child cross a busy road.

34 Rules of behaviour for teachers

Did you know that rules also apply to teachers? In the nineteenth century, female teachers had to obey rules like the ones listed below. Write out some rules you would like your teachers to obey!

Think about this!

Remember: rules should be for safety or to keep order. You might like to discuss some suitable rules for your teachers with the rest of your group.

Rules of behaviour

1. You must be home between the hours of 8pm and 6am unless attending a school function.
2. You may not loiter downtown in the ice-cream stores.
3. You may not dress in bright colours.
4. You may under no circumstances dye your hair.
5. You must wear at least two petticoats.

 **35 Devising rules of behaviour**

Use this sheet to draft some rules of behaviour in your classroom.
You might then set them out as a poster.

36 Devising rules of behaviour

Use this sheet to draft some rules of behaviour for your teachers.
You might wish to illustrate your ideas.

Write part or all of each of these quotations in your best handwriting. You might set them out as a poster for display.

"Many forms of government have been tried, and will be tried in this world of sin and woe. No one pretends that democracy is perfect or all-wise.
Indeed it has been said that democracy is the worst form of government except all those other forms that have been tried from time to time."

House of Commons, 11th November 1947

"I would say to the House, as I said to those who have joined this government, 'I have nothing to offer but blood, toil, tears and sweat.'"

House of Commons, 13th May 1943

"Never in the field of human conflict was so much owed by so many to so few."

20th August 1940

"To jaw-jaw is better than to war-war."

Washington DC, 26th June 1954

"This is the sort of English up with which I will not put."

Comment on people who went to great lengths to avoid using prepositions at the end of sentences

Think about this! Now find some quotations from one of your favourite personalities, or a character in a book. Remember to refer to when and where the statements were made.

Some words you should know

Write these words in alphabetical order. Then practise reading and spelling them with your partner.

legislative authority democratic bureaucrat politician statutory political authoritative govern legal legislation authorise statute democracy bureaucracy government

Title

Invent some words and write a definition for each of them.
Follow the style of the example below. Read the invented words to your
partner and ask them to guess what they mean.

*"Dontopedology is the science of opening your mouth and
putting your foot in it."*

Prince Philip, the Duke of Edinburgh

_____

_____

_____

_____

_____

_____

_____

_____

_____

Try to write, as quickly as you can, some rules for bike-riding and inline skating in the streets near your home.

Rules for bike-riding and inline skating

Think about this!

We often need to write very quickly. When we do so, it is often difficult to keep your best handwriting.
Did your letters still join?
Can your partner read what you have written?

Handwriting check 5:
"Celebration"

Write this poem in your best handwriting.

Think about this! You might like to illustrate this poem, putting the speech into speech bubbles above the pictures. Remember to change the punctuation.

I don't like weddings, not at all,
I find them just a bore,
At least, that's how it's always seemed,
When I've been to them before,
There's all those boring relatives,
That come from far and near,
Scoffing little triangular sandwiches,
And swigging wine and pints of beer,
Saying, "Don't the bridesmaids all look sweet?"
and, "Isn't it a pity,
That the best man's wearing two old socks?"
or "Was ever a bride so pretty?"
But I can't wait for Saturday,
To see Aunt Beryl's face,
'Cos cousin Cheryl's marrying,
A Thing From Outer Space!

Willis Hall

42 A wedding invitation

Set out an invitation card to the wedding in Willis Hall's poem "Celebration" (see sheet 41). Here are some ideas of how to set it out. Decorate the card, if you wish.

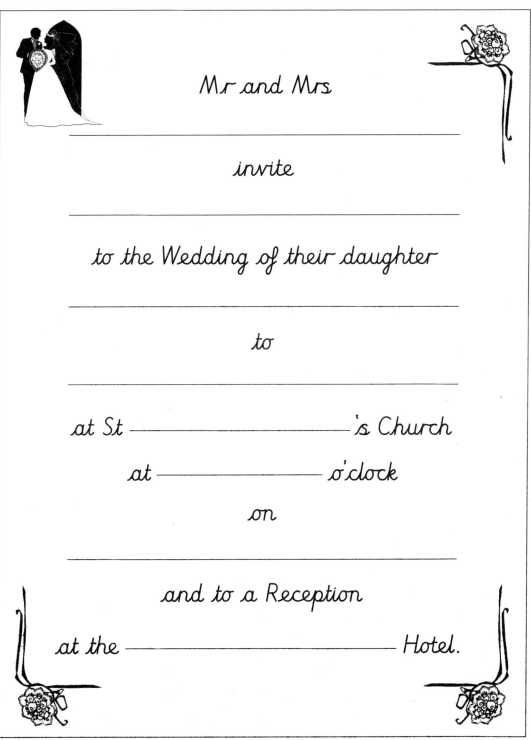

Mr and Mrs

_____

invite

_____

to the Wedding of their daughter

_____

to

_____

at St ——————————'s Church

at ———————— o'clock

on

_____

and to a Reception

at the ———————— Hotel.

Write these proverbs and sayings and then practise reading and spelling them with your partner.

Marry in haste, repent at leisure.

_____

_____

_____

_____

Faint heart never won fair lady.

_____

_____

_____

_____

One man's meat is another man's poison.

_____

_____

_____

_____

Where there's a will, there's a way.

_____

_____

_____

_____

All of these sports teams exist, and each has an unusual name.
Create your own unusual team names in the empty boxes.

Hamilton Academicals

Grasshoppers Zurich

Glenbuck Cherrypickers

Minnesota Timberwolves

Harlequins

Sale Harriers

Ipswich Witches

Think about this!

Would you use print or joined writing to write a team name?
Think about the logo and strip of your favourite team.
Design a badge or T-shirt in the correct team colours.
Think about the meaning of some unusual team names.

Famous quotations
(Sport)

Write some or all of these quotations in your best handwriting.
You might wish to illustrate your sheet with appropriate images.

"Boxing is glamourised violence."
Lord Taylor of Grufe

"There is one similarity between music and cricket.
There are slow movements in both."
Neville Cardus

"All you need to be a fisherman is patience and
a worm."
Herb Shriner

"Some people think football is a matter of life and
death ... I can assure you it is much more serious
than that."
Bill Shankly

"A horse is dangerous at both ends and uncomfortable in
the middle."
Ian Fleming

"You've got a goal. I've got a goal. Now all we need is a
football team."
Groucho Marx

"Golf is a game whose aim is to hit a very small ball
into an even smaller hole, with weapons singularly
ill-designed for the purpose."
Sir Winston Churchill

Use the first verse of this poem to begin your own three-verse poem about picking teams for a sport of your choice. Write your two new verses on the lines below.

Picking Teams

When we pick teams in the playground,
Whatever the game might be,
There's always somebody left till last
And usually it's me.

I stand there looking hopeful
And tapping myself on the chest,
But the captains pick the others first,
Starting, of course, with the best.

Maybe if teams were sometimes picked
Starting with the worst,
Once in his life a boy like me
Could end up being first!

Allan Ahlberg

_____

_____

_____

_____

_____

_____

_____

_____

_____

_____

Handwriting check 6:
"The Lady of Shalott"

Write this extract and assess how much your handwriting has improved since you began your handwriting folder.

Willows whiten, aspens quiver,
Little breezes dusk and shiver
Thro' the wave that runs for ever
By the island in the river
                Flowing down to Camelot.
Four grey walls, and four grey towers,
Overlook a space of flowers,
And the silent isle imbowers
                The Lady of Shalott.

By the margin, willow-veil'd,
Slide the heavy barges trail'd
By slow horses; and unhail'd
The shallop flitteth silken-sail'd
                Skimming down to Camelot:
But who hath seen her wave her hand?
Or at the casement seen her stand?
Or is she known in all the land
                The Lady of Shalott?

Only reapers, reaping early
In among the bearded barley,
Hear a song that echoes cheerly
From the river winding clearly,
                Down to tower'd Camelot;
And by the moon the reaper weary,
Piling sheaves in uplands airy,
Listening, whispers "'Tis the fairy
                Lady of Shalott."

Alfred Lord Tennyson